Municipal Love Poems

Also by Simon Smith

North Star
LEXICON
Night Shift
Juicy Fruit
Fifteen Exits
Reverdy Road
Mercury
London Bridge
Gravesend
11781 W. Sunset Boulevard
Half a dozen just like you
Navy
Salon Noir
More Flowers Than You Could Possibly Carry:
Selected Poems 1989–2012
some Municipal Love Poems
The Books of Catullus
DAY IN, DAY OUT
Last Morning
Source [with Felicity Allen]

Simon Smith

Municipal Love Poems

Shearsman Books

First published in the United Kingdom in 2022 by
Shearsman Books
PO Box 4239
Swindon
SN3 9FN

Shearsman Books Ltd Registered Office
30–31 St. James Place, Mangotsfield, Bristol BS16 9JB
(*this address not for correspondence*)

www.shearsman.com

ISBN 978-1-84861-822-0

Copyright © Simon Smith, 2022
The right of Simon Smith to be identified as the author
of this work has been asserted by him in accordance with the
Copyrights, Designs and Patents Act of 1988.
All rights reserved.

ACKNOWLEDGEMENTS

Some of these poems appeared previously in a selection published by the Muscaliet Press, as *some Municipal Love Poems*, and in magazines and anthologies. I offer my thanks to those editors for their time, generosity and attention:
*BOTCH, Litmus, Molly Bloom,
PN Review, Poetry Wales, Shearsman, For Robert,
Fugue and Subterfuge: A Festschrift for Alan Halsey,* and
The World Speaking Back: to Denise Riley.

'After Baudelaire: The Cygnet,' received a Special Commendation
in the '*PN Review* Translation Prize,' in 2017.

Cover image by kind permission of David Rees

Contents

GENERAL PURPOSE LOVE POEMS

General Purpose Love Poem	11
The Rhythm of Algorithms	16
Picture Window	17
Wavelength	19
Political Love Poem	21
Entertainment	24
Paris Traveller's Farewell Love Poem	25
Poem for Hipsters	27
Poem: Solo	29
Written With a Waterman	30
Personal Political Poem	31
Birthday Poem	35
Calling In	36
After Baudelaire: The Cygnet	37
Lines of the Poets	41
Homing	43
On Being Cis	45
Poem: In the Confessional Mode	47
General Pastoral Poem	50
Data Shadow Love Poem	51
Valentine One More Time	53
On Air	55
Poem After the End of Time	58
North Coast Exile's Love Poem	60
Angel Road	62
Interpretation Centre	64
Loop the Loop	67
Discarded Love Poem	68
Eleven After Eleven	71
From the Plains of Codeine	72
Poem: Listening	74
Another Political Love Poem About Love	75
Love Song: After Effects	77

SONG BOOK: SERIES OF SONGS

Song: Poem	81
Song: Final Touch	83
Song: For Rodefer	85
Song: Call Sign	86
Song: Throat	87
Song: Room	89
Song: Red Signal	90
Song: Turn	92
Song: Against the Light	94
Birthday Song	96
Song: Undertow	97
Didactic Song: Codeine Sonnet	98
Song: Valentine	99
Song: Interpreted	101
Song: Word	103
Song: Cloud	104
Siren's Song	106
Song: Oracle	108
Song: Call	109
Singsong	111
Song: Puzzle	113
Simple Song	115
Song: For Orpheus, After Rilke	117
Song: Poem	118
Political Love Song	119
Song: Charm	122
One Last Song	124

'I am only satisfied if my spectators, shivering and shuddering, raise their hands or cover their eyes out of fear of ghosts and devils dashing towards them.'
—Étienne-Gaspard Robert

'We have all become people according to the measure in which we have loved people and have had occasion for loving.'
—Boris Pasternak

For all those who were there along the way.

GENERAL PURPOSE LOVE POEMS

General Purpose Love Poem

this poem has passed the turn
cornered where it could be
a sonnet & twice as sweet

as fourteen pence of change
as fourteen sous of change
as fourteen bits all in a row

the fourteen lines of chance
& the six degrees of knowing

on London streets
along the boulevards of Paris

not an earthly
art without a heaven
not without chance

micrometer right
to the exact fit

& not without dance
Love is this logical

there's fun to be had out there
there there & there

waiting for the freebee waiting
for the end

of the barrel to settle
& sneak a half

there's a fizz in the glass
& the pleasure is mine
& ideological

like a guitar with L|A|N|G|U|A|G|E printed all along the fret board

not a cloud a note to a chord
to the mournful Doppler effect
of a passing ambulance

& empty talk empties song

my love is like a red
red rose after a skin full

a stretch from Tower Hill
a shuffle to the 'Cheese'
a cab to the Hole in the Wall

tonight the senses so light I could walk
through a wall
easy as that

phone emergency services phone

signal tied in knots
signal held in knots
calls held in queues

on the hop of Hope
on the post-it of Hotel Apostrophe

on the orchid petals like labia
    see
       that fits
& flits
no contact about the midriff

my one true love has disrupted the Time/Space continuum

sat on the Meridian

knocked wonky

her hair like fish bones
an earthly art beneath heaven

>	let's talk tax
>	let's talk sex

>	let's talk oral
>	let's talk talk

& walk
beneath me behind you

a black hole
to discourse

empty song empty talk
webbed in the freedom to disobey
grieving grievance since you're going

gone with
Baudelaire to Cimetière du Montparnasse
Rodefer to Père Lachaise

& her name on you
her kiss on you
healed

her overbite bitten
you a bit down at heel
victim's victim

leaning where others have leant
leant money clothes words
nettled

my reality a virtual reality near viral

they say Love is
netted in the discourse of someone named Astrid

that goes down with the empties & empty laugh

down the Thames
the insane Seine

& you need to watch your song
like a hole in the Universe

I don't complete surveys
or questionnaires or prize-winning draws
or mind the shop

Prosecco that bright & foolish wine
help ourselves to a second popping glass
a crop a season a vintage

my data shadow my soul

this fruit light of Africa & the Middle East
as more people walk away
to shadows & grit

Love is ideological
& swallows it all

down in one go
as a serpent dislocates
its jaw

in a theatre (Bataclan)
in a café (Bonne Bière)
in a bar (Le Carillon)

in a restaurant (La Belle Équipe)

the recoil
to this trembling moment

out of time
on the streets where Love is possible

The Rhythm of Algorithms

blackbird on the squeaky fence
Spring just round the corner
I'm guessing

a fragment a flag a flying
splinter

stop by the office about six
when you could be home
in what is said

of existing
in the fact
delight

is enough
daffs in a vase
bitten & burnt with age

or as I recall a sunrise 1968
facing West
dawn behind

between birth & death

as days sweep across the face of earth
axes x to y

Picture Window

& all the houseflies have dropped
well like flies
surely a sign

this is the tip towards the end
a husk
with a lot hanging by it

or off of it
the mind whirring out of control
like broken clockwork

the veer from ballistic to balletic to ballast
the lunge trip forward
subject to Baudelaire's shock tactics

the sun behind standing at the corner
with the poise of a hand
poised over the door handle

exit or entry

the question goes begging
with all the equipoise
butterflies carry throughout their lives

for a taxidermy of past feelings
like stuffed animals

signed off with a ballpoint
my thumb planted firmly over the evidence
there's to be no exception for others

politician parrot patriot or partisan
no one knows who's in charge

or to own the answer
like there is one

answer when there are answers

as we gather around another point
in history change pins swop phone numbers
exchange codes switch nations

of what remains

Wavelength

through the chorus
stressed or interested
someone's anemone

through the storms
where the song is located
under the 's' its places

expanding forever outward into its space
through its sound over its shadow
beyond its sonic boom

broader border borrowed
off an edge
a bridge

above the 's' its 'shuuuuush'
below its 'sssssss'
in the form of a sine wave

on the 's' of artifice
a semblance of balance
change under the tongue

everywhere alive above
out in the air
facing the sun

working things out
song reading all the way
back of echo

through the stones
the pulse the curve the breach

acres upon acres of empty
suspended floor space
energy jumps across

living space
charge under the tongue

to read the road
inhabit the language
pressings mouth to new

my voices with your eyes
word on a breath
when a mirror is a clock

all held back behind the tongue
the song
some future language

Political Love Poem

a breath turning sour
out there in the groves

of the hero
with human hair

where there's no enemy
& no memory side by side

where the heron takes its place
at risk of tipping the Universe
its step its stop to silence

lost to late Schubert
stylus & clouds

start up the hurdy-gurdy
the rich itch designed to consume
tap at the heart of the wind up song

turning outward beyond
the cold the light the high

spot to the music to the bit
bitten down along the bite
contour to counterpoint

the play too late for the lute
& too late to collect the loot

whose echo is not knotted
crumbled like chaff

dust inside the head
of a god

turning in the cutting wind

eyes burnt out of the stare
eyes burnt out of the star

heron composed as a suicide
poised to tip

forging base language
into pure song
into various song

drained of all energy but attention
certain as the white bark of silver birch

through connection
heart lifting
like radio

singing to silence
for when you can hear
the thinning edge

how do you read a desert
how do you read a heart
play it like a lute

counter & straight
look out into the broken broken broken

& all such things
that pass without incident
& high conversation

the wound up wind
wind down on the wound

the grooves
to blue hillsides

or further embedded song
to the lost edge

turning away into the Real
turning onward
whose echo

Entertainment

water surface at high tension
splash through the puddles

should do the trick
like magic

the financial markets fall down dead
drunk
in the manufactured salad

    SMALL (EMBEDDED) SONG

    Adorn   *o*
    Adorn   *o*
    Adorn   *o*

    three layers of blue
    on the politics in music
    sweet music

    sic musick
    sheet music
    useless app

dead as the tedium of Reality
T.V. & data
transfer

Paris Traveller's Farewell Love Poem

when 3G all the way across Paris is sluggish
& despair itself in the shape of a spiral
rests on that trope the cliché of clichés

add the serious waft of Givenchy
to the mix of bifteck moyen Beaujolais
the scatter of café tables & you'll draw your own picture

imagine Poetry as a service industry
to which the I as a voting member of the public has nothing to add

how odd city soundtrack sampled from this window seat
deafening rush hour trucks & buses & cars down long-gone tram tracks
the not-ideal Past where there's no going back to

to the bleak hotel rooms to sleep it off in defining bleak

what source for the lyric
& what not
& your tattoos obviously not 'my scene'

plastic wood added to '80s patterned curtain fabrics & carpets
powdered coffee powdered milk for all the world powdered

to sip the dregs of coffee
of all behaviours all possible experience
patterning thought patterning recall patterning

where any mobile vibrates close to a beating heart

to this beating heart all that beauty
in crepe paper in silver paper
coloured lights

is all the beauty beauty is

parading the Paris cemeteries by night
tanked on miniatures
snapped shut as a wallet

whilst the Little Boots of the new states of chaos
develops a taste for coffee
& Tweets at quarter of three

to be worn like a medal you fool
into the early hours lost to the dead time of bullets news bulletins
& the dead eyes of millions

sick for lyric
& rumour of the markets
& all the delusions of a freezing sweet white wine

as when I had the chance to call in you were out

in this the land of lost signals
of one last request one last meal
& the one last minute email

on all this Twenty-First Century Literature & all that's gone lists
rests & fails

Poem For Hipsters

email corrodes my soul
coat unbuttoned

nerves shot late morning
the same blue sky

before & after
symbolic as traffic clears

& the light fails & trails
under the badge of Love
the label of enchantment

speak to the Dead
not like Rilke
not likely like Rilke

but on the point of no return
pin on fun

shift & change down to the churning pool of Hades

to flush away the terrible night
a residue of ghosts

when those are poems finished as a ransom note

lodged somewhere between
the Baroque & the Sublime

I'll rewrite the lot
with night conversations

when the rest are grey
my enthusiasm runs ahead of me
a new poem dashed off

when the rest of the pack is cold
demotivated
won't play

frees my account with an up-to-date pin

more tired with ruined sight
caught in some vortex

of healthy rivalry spun round & up
he drove me nuts & out of Hope

we mourn our dead over the horizon

nowhere safe for sure
through the material world of blood ink paper

a creased postcard
buckle & dip
slipped away

ah one whose number I don't have
out of control
trying to call

Poem: Solo

retreat & exile a treat
of heroes & herons
a World full

& spills
splits resemblance

flips the Sublime into trash & everything
goes 'crunch'

in the pouring sun
when it might as well be driving rain

the grammar & syntax break off you
break you

& Life doesn't stop there
there or even there
the potency in potential

out of leaves like hands
like points of contact
like reason

you don't own the stylus
you don't own the moon

primroses amongst chalk boulders
open as receivers

when I exit to air
making the impossible possible
making home hum come to no harm

Written with a Waterman

like selling snake oil over the internet
hitch up to your personal trainer
I wouldn't change you for the news

when memory is where I live & love you still
& can't think off limits
I didn't know it then but these were my last moments

to take this line of thought further
a little bit like Dior scents the day

like heart bingo
maybe too Old World too quizzical maybe

or we could pretend we could
to true Mayakovskian decadence
& an early exit to Heaven

no other chat-up line will do
like when all I'm left with for friends
are those bad poets on Facebook

or pain a pin pinning pining in the pine needle
in the forest

    LOVE SONG

    this era of the unlovable
    love the unloved
    God is unlovable

when somehow somewhere something got serious
more smoke than mirrors
more woods than there are trees

for seeing substitute looking
a scallop roof

Personal Political Poem

personal poem taken personally
I'm trying to break your mind

with a poem I stay indoors with
stay home
I'm a stay-at-home dandy

I'm a black flag waving anarchist
I'm a passenger not an archivist

in a corporate research environment
you know I'm saying something that can't be trusted
& poetry is that occasion like a fire truck

when alcohol is the only thing that stops me being emotional
when the World Wide Web is our 'Arcades Project'

the slogan normal
for the transmission of emotion

when is it safe to cross on amber
when only the shape is left

the boulevards & the precincts empty
with nothing as apolitical as an angel
flattened against the sign of history

like a steamroller
generates a programme called 'STALIN'
& the eradication of the private life

crossing the road against the signal
for the public good
when being there is not enough

generates a programme called 'STAIN'
administers the daily dose of statins
& I am to be swallowed by a landscape

swallowed by information
& all this kink
no breeze no air no wind

between the Delphic Oracle and SunnyD
where none of the data is inconsequential or sequential
but on the mend

I'm a witness not an activist

as when something as inanimate as a poem

the whole world tips out of my iPhone

the dead boy washed up on the beach
the dead bodies of aircrew nudged along the Med
Homer's *Iliad*

beautiful people to the horizon
on some hideous poster
to the horizon

where the looking forward is now the looking back
back to letters

to obtain
leave to remain
folded into envelopes

beautiful purple smudge to the horizon
the perfect match
to step to

the template
the cutting out of consciousness
the cutting of conscience

& every moving part

as hideous doubtless
some Monsanto experiment
over the fields far distant removed

as some metaphor or some simile or graffiti
round a plain rude vase

I'm trying to break your heart with

a poem with *this* poem
(suggestible)

I'm a seer not an agent

as blue shadow when it moves to song
fresh as
water from the main

say I got it there first
fresh with its wetness
got it

say I got there first
with only radio for company
a new page of say so

a fresh page
says go

cast off like film spooling out
from a projector
out of time

out of control
& independent of exchange value

speckled with rain
I'm an echo not a sleeper

to sing or to say
this is how the Dead feel free

something as intimate as a poem

Birthday Poem

the distance each day you are born into
like the tree that came down in the storm

things are moving fast with the body's tension
how do you make the ordinary language sing

the intimate letters
of a poem
like petals

an anniversary folds memory under memory
between molecules
& the vast distances between planets

allows room for Love
living in daylight
& every second

the ocean reflects light back into Space
on itself

no one's eyes upon
nor returned home
memory is a room

years to step back from
& away there
clouds borne above

like the rainbow complete
above the hut & into another day
tipped forward

Calling In

ideology retired to private space
lets go the arrows
of fast answers & valentines

when airlifted to the next concept
I'm seeing different things

where the poems express emotion
I am now the coverlet of blown fragments
the degree of empathy poetic

tag along for the pain
where boundaries end
ditch whole criteria

that's where honesty gets us on the record

theories lie ahead or behind passing over

After Baudelaire: The Cygnet

1.

Andromache
my thoughts are with you

from a little trickle
poor & sad mirror of Ages ago
echo to your unbearable loss

now the sour Stour busted with your tears
shocking my teeming memory
into action –

from the close
dog's leg crossing Beaconsfield Road
then down the back alley

– recalled for me the new Carrousel –

old Paris is no more
sadly the shape of a city
switches to the quick of a heartbeat

as in a vision
I see improvised work camps

a jumble – a jungle in heaps
of rough-cut columns & capitals

– undergrowth overgrowing huge blocks
stone discoloured with verdigris
& all that

tangle of tat glitters from shop windows

right there a zoo spread out
right there one morning

at the chilly zero hour
a cold & clear sky

as Work rising from sleep
as the road workers
break silence with their din

a cygnet lost to its mother
its webbed feet flapping
along the dry road

dragging his white wings
across the roughened surface
beside the dried up drain

the poor thing beak wide

desperately thrashing its wings
in the muck
with a heart full

of need for his natural state
& element
hissed

"o water when will you rain down again
when will your thunder rip through Heaven"

I see that troubled bird
foreign & fatal myth

sometimes towards the sky
like Man in Ovid's tales

towards an ironic and punishing blue sky

raises his starving head
with a twist of the neck
to shout down God

2.

Paris changes
but my sadness
will not budge

tower blocks cranes
prefab concrete façade
all flipped to myth

& my memory weighed down more than stone

& so next to the Louvre
I am frozen by the image –

I recall my majestic bird
& his thrashing wings

with the exiles
ridiculous & Sublime

gnawed at by unending recollection
& then you

Andromache
tipped from the hero's embrace
a defiled chattel

in the hands of pompous Pyrrhus
Hector's widow wife of Helenus
Isis bride slave of Daesh

on BBC News 24 the emaciated woman
of colour – sick
from her odyssey

her bloodshot eyes staring vainly
through the murk

for the palms of Africa
not there

I recall all of them lost
who can never ever
reclaim what they've lost

those who drink their own thirst
in their own tears
like Romulus & Remus at the breast

& think of all children starved & shrivelled like flowers

*   *   *

here
in the dark wood
where I'm exiled with my mind

an old memory rings out the bells

& I think of all the mariners lost on a deserted island
of all the prisoners of all the desolate –
& of all the others

Lines of the Poets

name a name
at one point in history

named a boulevard a square a circus
before the others got bored
packed up went home

[clear my throat]

most of my poets are dead poets
most of my lines are dead lines

something of the everyday
like the grit in the oyster
vague whiff of beauty among the clichés

language carries all hope
& there's work to do

& I've come around to that line of thinking
with too many moving parts
as new arrivals roll off the train

one more of them
Baudelaire the poster boy of Modernism

& the time of boredom
¾ a poem within a poem:

> *AFTER-LIFE*
>
> *living the after-life*
> *living in the after-life*
>
> *I dance on my legs*

down on my knees for it

there are procedures
some of them legal

& pure animal product
resolved into a book
of numbers

a flux
a film
a mist

Homing

head hollowed out

no one sweats opposite the mirror
the freshened tap water & cut flowers
like terms of reference

to tremble at the border another
beautiful day & another borrowed

the enchanted commonplace
is not to transfigure but embody
is to wrap the wound of seeing

particles of language part
in patterning

field after field after field
posted posts into distant distance

air full of swifts air full
shade among shade
& Love

blooded roses & carnations
a cut glass vase

shape listening to you
shadow

twisted over like a dream
read off a phone

leaves hiss the song
a house in the country rowan berries

the first
the wind & the turn

the landscape its own song
air & light full
tilt

a house in the lowlands
a pigeon feather
seesaws to ground level

so-called border control

without music
& the flags are falling
hollowed out head

On Being Cis

& who are they speaking for
the music at the top of the World
could cloud cold

like propellers or flowers carry plenty ID
sipping black coffee
above the terraces

my head a rush of memory or geometry
provided the tipping point

as to where & when you decide
to switch off the life support

there's a branch line & you've said it
shut up chat up
the flower shop opposite

& head or ping towards inky darkness
the vile vial of ink

& suddenly we are to be
released into the network
of exchange

free of will or free will
its at that moment I feel

the need to be folded
in your arms like a cliché

it's a gesture no one cares for
dropping off the stool
or spilling out of the taxi

for every penny
eyes itch I rise to my feet & shout

to the angle of self-destruction
the crucial angel

the man who knows what genius is is the man who knows

cruelty
rhapsodic & icy
trembling lost to opportunity

Poem: In the Confessional Mode

this poem could be mine
hard & real as this tabletop

[knock knock]

fine as finest finessed
accurate as sunlight falls against a door

enough metaphor is enough
to step back from as
too much Depeche Mode is a lesson for us all

& many a lost mojo
in the light of a controlled recce
& the bluest Blues

is to be knocked back on track

in the class of disappointment
where the work
of one's contemporaries

just does not ring
true
does not sing does not

he does odes he does
bright as a crime scene
the corner shop floodlit

her twinset blown open
guts splayed

open to cold inspection & marble slab
& the coroner
in the TV detective series

or a 21st Century Baudelaire
louche studied mannered Boho
leans against a door jamb

shopping for cheap vodka
& weed

browses Northern European towns
like a tourist

the satellite dishes tilt
dip into sun like sunflowers
& follow all routes

to the end of the ether
to be populated

text algorithms & space junk

silk air sea
cargo along lanes trails
trade routes

& unhinged lyric

of news report in its shell
& bullet
the mercy of friendly fire

& round-the-clock bombing
wrap around warfare fully industrialised
sound falling

with shells & chemicals & shards

more unlike song I cannot imagine

o lament
o melody
o memory

licked gum along the flap to a manila envelope
along the hinge
to sealed memory & a different fingerprint

to what I say
beak wide
sings out

General Pastoral Poem

East Anglian prairie
virtual & abstract
cubed

the feeling of home stopped
all of a sudden

the Andrew Wyeth glance back
curbed as memories
sit out the afternoon

as the sun rushes forward west

straw bales packed tight
lime-green furze to each branch

Nature & landscape
the difference between
touching Spring

pallets stacked as far as the eye
yard by yard

the financial markets fall over dead
as ash die back
added schadenfreude for tedium

Data Shadow Love Poem

announcing anyone
of importance

streets named after soldiers
kings politicians

where have all the poets gone
off the cliff's edge

the brown & shrivelled leaves
of Baudelaire
tossed along the railway siding

blue skies mottled cloud to shrieking gulls beyond car alarms

on the button
of now

you've gone further
I can't speak to you

looking in the wrong place for the wrong thing
gone too far

this time
without recourse to favour
or entitlement

images mostly at night move on
where *polis* becomes occupation

dead-eyed from scrutiny & assessment
beta blockers unravel the synapse

from daily aging is a kind of grief
a sliding off the edge of the earth

the edge of asphalt yellow hieroglyphs
demarcate where to dig next

pigeons whirr & circulate
like turbines in the act
of flight

between plan & innovation
between chimneys & terraces

to huddle to one hot spot
& float up to my office
hit the one dead spot

we could call it quits
the x+y marry male to female

how we knot the knot of discourse
float about the day
to shimmer like a poem

over the fence
of constellations in some states

over some managerial role play
or another at the bestial end
of the delirium spectrum

you're nowhere without Baudelaire in your back pocket
the absinthe of God in the absence of God

Love profiled
a pin-prick of moon
a spoonful of moonshine

Valentine One More Time

walking along an open road
duffle-coat done up the neck
collar up against the cold

midway February
Love look where it goes
before you

check the stars
where even rocket science isn't rocket science
the rest is flesh and crossed threads

like to like & Alpha Centauri
between snow drop & hellebore

& it will be & it will be & it will be
your breathing says
'I know where all the stories are buried'

as the Milky Way shifts about like a shower cap (or God)
to where all the rockets fall in a great sigh

like arrows
keeping time too much in love
for the World to die

my heart is mauve
a marketing opp for *Hallmark*
a marketing app for Apple

lost in the joy of things
the lost joy of things
lost the joy in things

when is a tourist a terrorist
when the nightclubs are full of the Sublime

my heart a shade
your heart pill-box red

a quadratic equation
out on the mountain of oblivion
what the words lean on

what the moment does is a song where I don't think
to live with the Dead over the horizon

On Air

when under song under sound
where the poetry machine carries on
as normal carries as bystander

or in the heart before language

when I exit to air
where I exist

as though nothing is
happening with nothing
to see nothing

as you talked your way
into this precarious moment
of attention

to stride away over rivers & mountains
crowds of crows mark journey into exile

ache all in song

impressions
incoming become thick & opaque

shaken wakeful halfway through
awake too awake to

dodge doorway to doorway
between showers

how witness is political
looking on on looking
signs & omissions

& the flags are falling without music
tilting towards the high end
of daylight

sky overcrowded by air lanes
& vapour

I turn in the dark next to you
we enter
the death phase

next as air rushes through endless unnamed cities
as tons of water through dead ocean

above the burnt out tower above
killing time
in a name in a home

the helicopter whirl circles
circles again circulates air
then off

crashes journey into exile
crushes through & rough

shows signs bent towards forward
coming at one bright instant

I go with you now
in the churn

what instructs underneath
poetry floats above
language

where the heart appears before
wrapped all in a song
endless as tides

poetry is the enemy of the people
conversation discourse between equals
to ache with politics

to squeeze the air out
a sun of yellow showered light asunder

make the mark
screening data capture

in the ache the risk
at the heart of

said aloud into cloud above
roughened air

or speech
bubble

crow to crow post to post
Spring fresh & green & unravelling

in shadow
in my sleep

in this language
in this turn
is politics

Poem After the End of Time

it's when I see a shape it comes
marks its arrival
& the politics are your call

while the destruction of the World grinds away

she had the aura that broke me
& if I can't have you then I'll fill the page

because
Time no longer exists
History no longer exists

Politics no longer exists
extending into the endless future
heat wave floating in off the ocean

& that's the Law
we all lay down in

in the present climate everything takes on a new shade

pours out & scrap all 'Culture'
I mean pressing hard
pressing forward

as images twist in the air

past the tipping point crowd into mob
the demagogue knows his Lenin
& the politics have eaten my tongue

as a naked man drinking coffee
I am swallowed by a bed

the maid singing in the next room
sweet & truly anonymous

all to herself
in all its political agency

it is the time to step
back a step
turn out of my depth

beats hard upon the tongue
when its best to keep an eye

on all the colours
of all the hundreds & thousands

when all the poem can do is wriggle
listen outside the musical pattern
with it

speak Truth to sing
my heart in ashes
alive between everything

what I'm saving all my human teeth for
from my particular little corner of the World Wide Web
when I've spent the day in orange socks

its as though to step through the mirror
to the side of the Dead

when fill a page will not do
the trees form a kind of lettering

an area an aura an era
lost sight of

when the debris floats by the window
then there's the call to signs

North Coast Exile's Love Poem

throw it off & move to the coast
rural idyll & listen with new ears

sipping un demi-tasse a half glass
toasting my dears

below a certain temperature the red
tastes a metallic blue

the full pitch of the marketing team behind
with all the power to sell
before I switch to The World Tonight

I'd better plonk another log on the fire
pick about the bag of coal with tongs

left with a mouthful of ash
blasted by Arctic winds in April
like I'm February's dead wood

so into the top oven you go ready-made or takeaway
sitting in waiting for the swallows
to swoop down across the gloom

a dripping tap
regular as an atomic clock
at the pips

tell me memories
can't be tipped out of chaos

my later years cramming the page
whizzed by to Bill Evans' 'Autumn Leaves'

all this (& more) swamped in estuarine despair
like chopping wood with a hairbrush

through air
by road for an overnight stay
whilst we nibble round a corpse we call a meal

the all-of-a-sudden shockwave overhead
pipes me aboard a higher plain of consciousness

dive-bombed into submission
by the boys from Lakenheath

bring me their F15s their F111s
out of the camouflage of a clay-grey sky
tracking the coastline

tilt at the impossible angle the angle of angels

the pennywhistle tune
of Valkyrie through the intercom

a kind of circuits & bumps
a full-blown fly past

trooping the colour
misplaced loyalties
borne out of atrocities

to the tune & precision of a drone
viscera degraded/denigrated to myth
flips over a snail into a snarl

Angel Road

I look upon you with utter delight
that's my job

operating well in excess of recommended safety levels

halo/hallo/hallelujah
my life of distractions

caught on the entry camera
is to have no memory is to have
no enemy

this is a Love poem
in the poem's embrace that loves the World
like a new (invisible) planet

beyond
unnamed cosmic dust
there all the days of humankind

& more
in my life of distractions

in series
in this envelope between
earth & stratosphere

twelve miles high
crash out stay put
therefore this poem doesn't exist

the place of removal
thinking things out
thinking things through

thinking things
I don't know why when
it all feels wrong

there's no moving forward
& how I miss you & howl
symptoms synapses

& signposts through the eyes
buds to statistical analyses

conduct oneself with grace is the goal
as a line of poetry

a flower on the mouth

Interpretation Centre

& the first question I have to ask
is the first of simple things

you don't want to answer
or find answers to
is like penance

how to resist
what to resist
why resist

how can I sit here
& with the clouds
listen to the sea

in navy & marine
what flag do I fight under

diamonds hearts clubs spades
flying like pennants

all along the coast
container ships tankers
at anchor

I buy an umbrella
as talisman against the wind
& the rain

& crunch of shingle & ballast
something wrenched from its fittings in this weather
something metallic heavy something ballistic

locked out scripted
with your track record
embedded

degraded shell
mother of pearl

answers are anchors
drag the seabed
instead one sits through the days

& records of insane record-keeping
authentic pop booming blood through
inner ears

a little knocked sideways
blue paint written on in red

presents in the shape
of soap & spades
procedure & order long gone

the signal decay without purchase
a slow turn

o bluish bruise
at the sight & at the sign
of flesh tones

crown & anchor

if you can't measure it it doesn't exist

& the promise to keep your mouth shut
in the shallows of first thinking

over the cliff-top walk
of soft sandstone

thoughts' clarity
winter's thought
in wintry air

the question home
half asleep one

eye on my work email
pearl within shell

Loop the Loop

what hangs by a thread
footage that's what

the power field of the first sentence
break off
leave for the continent

in the shadows of first thinking
syntax for facts & content

    ARCH FOR ANGEL

    I don't know why when
    it all feels wrong
    there's no moving forward

    & how I'd miss you & howl
    symptoms synapses

    & signposts through the eyes
    buds to statistical analysis

content of the continent
flat as a glass of water
is as it is

natural causes the air
dull & thick & closed

Discarded Love Poem

Lunch Poems hanging out
of my back pocket
the way *Kapital* never could

but in all truth where does it go
when in all truth where does that leave you
part company with no choice

living the dream which is only another hour
onward & a kind of nightmare that's where

or objectively the crux

where we ask too much of knowledge
where does all that Truth get us

& drops a spanner in the works
in the allegory of commodification
of representation

with the effect of the affect of everyday life

from the sea-grey sofa cast adrift
a raft of afternoons to drift out on
sunny after grey fresh after close

muggy after chilly
& that's the weather resolved

but what's left
insoluble in the rain

lost like a mirror's forgetting
a poser like a desert

which the more intimate
the more innate
the more to imitate

when I'm paralysed brain up
when all I repeat miss you

miss you miss you miss you
over & over & over & over
again penetrates right to the heart

so says the telegram
from the closed-down seaside town

on the tilt towards me noodling around
& through a sugary light
rest the eyes

forget the rest
various multiple somethings
we all fall foul of

on the boring trudge across suburbs
the dormitories cars parked
neatly on drives

& all the other thoughts we had no need of
like the trunk of a silver birch like polished bone

or micro-beads & melting glaciers deactivating oceans
that are in need of the closest attentions

uncoupled from the break between showers
made from daylight in the shape of a song
or locked into speech acts

is to do a kind thing in transit
of thought process

like fixing
words as nails to wood

puts the putty in the filler
or vise versa toe to toe
the positive to the negative charge

& various outcomes as various
multiply multiples

these are not my people
no not for Love

& everyone home for the evening
like roosting gulls or parakeets

across the water a milky light
lit distant loci
locate floating continents

like content
to a strong suit
to a suite of multiple choices

or separate occasions
stick or slip stop or move

Eleven After Eleven

drowsing to Debussy's 'Images' from the stereogram
beneath three shades of blue

air still as a cormorant
prehistoric bird
feathers like scales

rainbow oil on tarmac
oily sheen running along the harbour

(insert) headphones switch to 'La Mer'
stroll along the marina
project a stratagem

infinitely reflected images

bobble & topple of saltwater
heavier
than the bobble & topple of freshwater

From the Plains of Codeine

flipped receptors opened synapses
the World is numb aligned next to me

in the coffin
cheek by jowl

functioning zero moral perspective

I can no more operate machinery
than you can write lyric poetry

ranks of emergency vehicles parade the boulevard tonight

in a World where the long term is now the short term
& Life is mostly experienced as pain
& Love is a payday loan

so the answer will always be "no"
like a kid's earworm

when the crowd's a rabble
& the constitution designed for the musket ball
drops down another communication black hole

it's a lottery the reckless belief life will carry on as it always has

where the thinking touches where it fits
& yes that makes it a wrap

the pain connected hot wire to the elbow
& the full dose of soluble aspirin over 24 hours
just won't do

all my clothes are secondhand at least twice removed
codeine friendly
the Naproxen years flip signification

& reading poetry off of my iPhone is the best place for it

the Angel of History pressed against the double-glazing

intoxicated in the code of codeine
& all the World stopped breathing

so walk out of the hotel
turn left
end up in Spain

the money turning into evidence

where I've kept your love as a kind of app
singing the heart inside out

reduced to a lone figure in a restaurant
in a restaurant not a café

where the line break is everything
& it's the Dead who run the show

Poem: Listening

I'm a cosmonaut not an astronaut
step out of the capsule

like steps in my diary
the lyrics I should have known

all this & the cosmos of daily living
listening listening always listening

air frozen to cockpit skylight
lyrics a cloudy foamy lemonade
orbiting the dream like a Surrealist

the language taut around the teeth
politicians talk it to the mob
I speak it to you you you & you

either by candlelight or fission
etched onto the wall like shadow
like soot or echo

or lyriks I should have worn out
like skirts like trousers or blank space

the song lags
& you're there always owning this

Another Political Love Poem About Love

where does all that Truth get us
laurel moulded to the brow
leap & lip that's where

we live for others if we live

my chest flooded
with breathless heartbroken struggle

a cosmic echo
reduced to a pulse
in the shape of an angel

of so many colours the body full
phantasmagoria
too much the cause of some interim hum

just for once there needs to be complexity
to lurch backwards in time

haul home the shame of those who didn't
either win or take part
in the twilit light popular as a lab rat

a workman hugging his hi-vis
rucksack to his chest
like an infant

rendered
homeless

takes the bullet
like a torn off stub

from China
the turn around of goods in thirty-six hours
shipped from the U.S.

product of China
owned by a multinational
of stateless ownership

transaction tagged
to all experience stored as information

there is to be no more now now

to swop adoption for adaption
& exile

my body full of shock
to be follower not leader
fair dos & hand-me-downs

reduced to mud
creased & flawed

& the man who always smiles for the photograph
calls it a day
enough is enough

sat helpless hands left over right
letting it happen
I have bees as you have heroes

a body full of colours

Love Song: After Effects

retro-yellow as a phone directory
I speak in my genuine voice
go forth in authentic threads

the tilt towards what will do
as what will show

for Love
looking in the wrong place
for the wrong thing

at the wrong time
which could be side-effects
or a flower of the mouth

or a political love poem
(tentative)

this is the time to discuss
& the time to sing
displacement

something of the lineage to cough
timeless as a jam-jar sprouting jasmine

when if we can't make things
then we'll sell the air

or ox-eye daisies or dog-rose a meadow full

the what-can-cause-you-harm
ease your pain
trying not to become another casualty

you recount instances of your biography
like a novel
like cut-outs

when twenty years ago is yesterday
composite & component

in keeping to another life & its entry-phone
I'm the one listened to by the myth

I'm the one written by the myth
where clichés click over into sound bites
pick up a badge or two

controlled by the trope
strafed by the strophe

the drone
of what might lurk
around the corner

the flip to say it better
its not too late

that we're at the end of time & possibility

there are smarter bombs
& other forms of market definition
like being stood in the path of a switch

swift & elegant with nothing to report
a sky unloaded of moisture
the speaking is difficult

not the speech
or the contemplation of objects

the interval between showers
the way you go before you flip into me
when it's all about showing up at the party

SONG BOOK: SERIES OF SONGS

Song: Poem

background
against the noise
something goes

then here
the replies flood in
on bent postcards

small somethings
steal some time
disappearing

like a pin

of light down
the back
of a t.v. set

never close

an answer
an eternity

of collared doves
where debris
is lodged by mistake

Byzantine lyric
long into night

deep Time
Iceland & celandine

replies farmed
tattered email

the storm of forever

rippling your coat
night into night

dissolve into &
out of light

to build out of nothing
the words set down
clean & still

clear as day
questions & noise
& what it means

to be alive
long into song

Song: Final Touch

& the things that matter
nightingales
steel girders olive trees & the like

like sound
waves like
radio waves

quite happy in my DNA
the miracle the ordinary
word on the breath & space

& the World inches forward
halfway
light in all directions

munching on speech bubbles
rain speckled light
emerge to blue & sun & cleared air

the same place via a different route
hearing the World through
the rough

intense dust bodies of water
shadows of cloud
weighted with stones

& the other things that matter
walking north
gaze switched on to capture

note
a place the sight of somewhere
never looked on again

the wind swerves
forever catches up forever
centuries of murder & terror beneath

or in a storm whiteness
in tears
in stars

looking for the sign
faded

like a flight path
& touch

Song: For Rodefer

tip the billycan
& now I should be gone
into sentimentality

the blown colours of Technicolor
Kodachrome
reds & yellows

Lone Ranger Flipper Batman
endless matinees
of Saturday Westerns

brighter with age
nudged out of shape
forge & forage whatever for

but percolate the butt
my notebook buzzing
like a smart phone

I can't help being allergic
to cant & the Sublime
as a Life-choice

or cloud
left under
rinsed at the coastline

the grand canyon
of a distant milky light

Song: Call Sign

you step off
the coastal route

to a low glow
& receive the call

like a dragonfly
broken panes for wings

red Saharan dust
on the airwaves

a thin film attaches itself
the jamb to that
dusts the limbs

& out to sea
the airmen cry
as refugees drown

a bluebell sheen
to fill with bluish light

once set in the past
unchangeable
& no return

run out of track
& representation

rooms without windows
or clocks
like a grey interview under strip-light

plus the black box issues its single pulse
from the seabed of the Med

Song: Throat

song the final line
of resistance

of what lies
behind the days
pianissimo

song all in
depth of field
& things to add to

the cloud speaks the rain
its conversation

do you need language before you
need the heart

in reverse
sunlight through the leaves
correspondences

sleep dream underscore
like chance & lies
the song like rain

passes through the lower registers
tawny & drab as a little bird

home in a name
amid the sound

building work
the bird mute

at dusk it could be dusk
copy of a copy

read
like a feather & hurt

the crowd another country
turns to song as it arrives in your head

carries meaning sound carries

a tune backwards
to boom & pick up

a thousand windscreens
as the surface of a lake

era & error
engulf all in sight like a death star

as a lost last ghost ship
threat to throat

Song: Room

still speaking silence
bodiless with voice

Angel the what-is-
lacking

path to the doorway

the lyric machine
in given motion
immortal & exhausted

the cold in the wound
head shredded

at the fold
memories remembering memories
as a flower might dream

when things do not
bodies pass

space legislated for
of newsprint & less resolution

when things get broken off the edge
retrieved as song

creasing light at ever increasing rate

Being in the saying
the always leaving left

Song: Red Signal

everything-hangs-on-a-thread
of one of those days
felt to the end of the glove

the Truth
sings as well as speaks
as nobody thinks about nobody

thinks about thinking
& not a thought

in this the land
of the last lost field
of dust & emptiness

of Sundays & recession
& daytime telly

live each day in the cliché
like it's the law
& Life's its vibration

pine table blue-stained
as a Spring sky
solid as solid

(not in the simple simile way
not in the thingness of metaphor
the haunt of poets

but in the tail light flicker
at the top of the hill
indicating right

repeated across traffic
redded in chinagraph

anonymous as lipstick
on a fairytale
looking-glass)

to break with what comes before
something mundane as a pigeon

something that goes to the heart of things
sets off the tremble
in the twilight light

Song: Turn

breathe
on the out breath
the song turns

the dance in attendance
in the turning turning
the thin edge

always sound assembled
to a screech

in the shadow of the shape of it
the share of it in the sharp
ledge

slumped towards the lower registers
shaped to the cut-out of song

this frozen earth
account unknown
encounter foreclosed

the way the Universe goes

when it goes
to show the foreseeable

calling to the end of the earth
when the World is slender a slender
slender thing

like a heron stood to attention
at the elbow of the eave
poised as a suicide

this slender air
a kind of accident
who & echo

in despair in disrepair
this slender air
in the blue the blur

like light aircraft drift in late after hours
props feathered

in the glance up
a reassembled trace

counter to nation
song swallowed to a shriek
& a knock on the door

calling in the shouting out
no such thing as the idea of free rain

Song: Against the Light

a blackbird drowns out the dusk

away to the infinite interior
down through every cell germ atom
& out

dispersed migrant

ragpicker side-
step sidereal
timing to absorption

to works & days
antique & obsolete

> *o a new box of tricks*
> *seeps*
> *the long game one off*

whilst I'm the sitter
away to the contingent studio
the gate goes unfixed the floor unswept

how much can the body do
with paint with weight

> *& out*

silent drive to the blue dusk light

collapsed with the event horizon
listening through the night to B sides
stride about the beet fields

when Life is all a question of budgets
& that is all

I'm hi on the World & the timing
the itinerant light
painting the acute air

the empathetic
long lines of blinds
sort out your face

better call the Director of Communications
the blackbird singing away
at the end of Time

> *clever dark little song*
> *call & response*

Birthday Song

the tree that came down in the song
living in the daylight

for which there is no use for
where the language is before
this envelope of light

in a leaf's song
in a lover's letter

Song: Undertow

pull
lack of control
until

currents encircle
legs
tipped up

wrapped round
winded inside the heart

lived entirely
in the touch

breath turn
folded back
of breath

turn
upset
out in the strand

love the unloved ground
song of the broken

low below low
watermark

the rain pouring
no singular thing
touch with wind

song how to go on
how to move on

the afterlife
with the signal breaking up

Didactic Song: Codeine Sonnet

read everything as beauty & you'll come to no harm
skip down the road or street
from memory until now

the box to put Love
& all the other non-paid work

this poem
this postbox of the Cosmos

I am what I ate
& will be

& am not
in code encoded
breathtaking the heart stopping

breathe in the codeine air
buy all the shares in water

Song: Valentine

walking along
an open road
walking alone

the sun adazzle
midday February

not my poem
but your song

inside
a beating heart
for you

a listening puzzle

the snow
the hail
the sleet

the rain all winter
at once

the rockets are falling
in a great sigh of rockets
into growling winter

heart & heart
pulse
side by side

bump bump
bump bump
bump bump

sounds like simile
after like

sweet weeds are these
& seeds

where your heart is
moving the light around

like razzamatazz & the Sublime
there's a paintbrush full

as the poem goes
this poem is yours

as all History
rushes forward
into this moment

a new Spring
behind the sunrise

would be to be
done with the World
we see the future

Song: Interpreted

without the Sublime a world of focus groups
without music in a life to wave a flag

the light of the next day
beneath breath

left with the echo
song quits silence
above soundings

above meaning
sail like a wing a wave
a wave pattern

a dove's wing above
utility above wing tips
tilts & twist

turn a ghost
a husk of hurt
& heart sound

Be everywhere point of contact
every detail is to track
a flutter the soft blow

moment between words
where song fails
& meaning falls away

drops away the veil
mist tips down the hill

of each passing moment
squeezed in the wind

aspire & identify
on camera
in drone capture

gone

Song: Word

if you never hear another word from me then this is the one
precarious as Heaven & as precious

back it up with looking
through the trees
look up into the trees for Truth

something to provide the light
touch

proof of bluebells
marked with no one to look upon them

a sheen of blue light
rising from woodland mulch

why resist

extinction why exist
one day you're feeling it
the next day you're not

what are the odds of that
& no comfortable position

when the Truth won't help you through the next extinction event

except accept the light touch of light
is like finding our choices

in the amber
cracked skin or epidermis

is like frayed nerves quietly monochrome
or other such minutiae melancholy or mundanity

Song: Cloud

that a cloud could be
how a house becomes

an extension of this body
its muck & dust

this fractured song
all its abstract beauty

the error you walk toward
it's a hard look
testing twisting

work towards error
lost the shine to chance

in that hard look
bone cold
greedy for the mornings

we are not gods

but aspire to close the door
not come back

the cloud over
dim amber light

singled out
then fewer

no less alive
throughout the day
heard in the faintest particles

collapsed into a bluish tinge
dipped in & out of doorways

lost to wherever
you're going I'm elsewhere

refuge in song
human error

ghost to my name
balanced above milky light

in the act I rang ahead
the song embedded

Siren's Song

the goods the secrets
dropped out of you
chilly

standing half of me
here half of me
unknown

so it comes down
again to the blue dawn
with rain

like gulls like sirens
like school children

blue light pirouettes
through night
an echo to the sleeper

the sound of children
at play
a playground full & their minders

waiting to enter this poem
a playground tipped to this moment
forever waiting

the signal is like an angel
in these last hours I see straight

to the tree line
to the horizon
through you

seeing things
for the last time
maybe

light like light

singing them
into existence
through blue exhaustion

Song: Oracle

inhabit the language
illuminated as several circular
arguments later

like linked sonatas
blown out on the ether
earth breath each breach

what disappears behind the moon
obstacle into shadow what disappears
word in a breath

when is a mirror a clock
when it follows a river
tastes like forever

all you've ever had is all
you've ever sung

Song: Call

nightingale calls
its burble ambush

to the jug
the jug for the trick
& pop

hitting the note
hitting the rain

its tempo
temporary
over overflow

is not what it says it says
what it sings is
the hot & the cold of it

locked to the sun
beginning with the ocean

the meaning & the patterning
the last & the lost
of earth settled up

cupped hands
for hearing
for water capture

butterflies programme the music
blue fills

the horizon
& audience close to chaos crowd mob
the jug the jug

away to night

INTERNAL NOCTURNE

*the moon full
cold with white sunlight*

as a sealed unit
lyric
logic illuminated & single

INTERNAL LOVE POEM

*my look is your look
a skin of light
your yoke*

lyric sprouting like a leaf
lyric reads like a landscape
blue without mercy

like a dream
like a complicated thing
square cloud of no doubting

speech bubbles of the crowd
expand fill burst

the politics
in the ticks of language
in the hum of song

Singsong

read a landscape
back into a lyric
into a lyre

missing a glass of water
where sound is to song

singsong
the strong suit

opening the side gate
to soundings & songs

of that bloody nightingale
a suite
& the music of sound

the phrasing of useless plastic
loot the song

lute to song
tunes into tomorrow
in its out of the wayness

out of the way
tune into today

tinnitus like alarm bells

is the opening of the day
the opening of blackness

out & out of out
of me

is there a reason
give me a reason

the rest is landfill
dragged flat
a source

of full disclosure

Song: Puzzle

the place where others gather round
a plan or map

in passing
to vanish behind the varnish

lyric you are my liar
when I'm talking to you

stops in my diary like a fishbone
or the same step tilting toward

forward by that logic
might be my last contact
or not

as leaks turn
into leads
hands deep in pockets

eyes sore with witness
to the footfall of the daily cosmos
own this & you're there

in the language you are
my lawyer
grammar & syntax

all along the breastbone
deep bass
of ragged telephone wire

& air
a blockhouse no horizon

T.V. aerials
without much to offer the crowd of angels

unpicks my lyre
of silver & dream

in song meaning
less
straightening out

when it's a beautiful day & you should be here in it

Simple Song

caught out
by the blue sheets of rain

dalliance or alliance
in the colour red

the secrets in the song
birds tell us
the endless

change of the guard
knocked off balance

wave
after wave

addressing the crowd
become a mob

out of rain
then into shadow

affected by the affective voice
mortal in the sentence

your breathing like sonar
tipping forward into the endless

difficult to read
& not weep

woken to song
brisk as a punch

automatic crack or
bang of a door

or the tidal cycle
cut out of the rain

cooler than colour
light ordinary
antidote to the anecdote

slip back
to my own piece of sky

take instruction
go to a room & write
go home in a name

curtains drawn music down
sing & lift

Song: For Orpheus, After Rilke

A god is capable. But enlighten me, how can
a mortal squeeze in between the strings of a lyre?
His mind in two. Where two tracks of the heart

twin, a temple for Apollo is impossible.
Song, the way you teach, is not longing,
not the weaving of the means to the end.

To sing is to Be. Simple to a god.
When shall we *Be*? And when will *he*
turn the earth and the stars on to us?

Boy, its not the 'being-in-love,' even though
you sing out, of your own accord – understand,
trash those silly love songs. They're gone.

To sing true is another kind of breathing.
Breath for no reason. Air within a god. A jet stream.

Song: Poem

the razzle dazzle do of now
with Wyatt my passport
frayed at the edge

my code
to this transport of Love
roses peeking over a dry-stone wall

the breeze the perfect
'fit' to body temperature

delight in the delight
the immanent imminent
incumbent

like Beauty is to Truth
like Life is to Death
like Rock & Roll

its all in the voice
you know
personal

up close as a signature
& a long lung
(with Whitman along too)

Life is song the body singing
shed like pollen like dust

what if the song were democracy
sung into being
commonplace

all the young people in a hurry
to start in green & end in blue

Political Love Song

when all we're worried about is content
in the creases of light
folded regular patterns about

the house
as shadows pass into another day
listen to a mirror

its regular signal
as a wave
backwards

which is where we are
the plummet down a crevasse

conversation
mountain

to find the words to live in

if its not too late
to be dragonflies sunning
tilted towards the sun

is what to do
& slowly

if only enter
pleas please if only

where time does not
follow loss

footfall
heard in the particles the faintest
neatened up

shut off locked on
gaze exchanged over time
I found the words we live in

the words in lives
in the shelter of shadows away from light

like a tear in the Universe
like radio

a flower of the mouth

you speak me
as if I were you which I am
where the footfall falls

complete as the cut-ups
where the Real lifts into abstract
some form of attendance

emergence from meeting
Love if you like

is not to live at the level of exclamation points
all energy concentrated to a private place
dwelling

its as listening to a puzzle
to murmur mutter
mirror

the present politics
mean you don't need to

to stop at the STOP sign
or any other
post

meaning
true to that word
emergency

in song

at this end of winter
relief from a cold snap
when at the door

a snowdrop nudges free

feeling unresolved
& solid

Song: Charm

here at dusk & now
how Heine's little songs
most of the time timing

close to tears
adrift
glad of the walk

take whiskey for the burn
not the shock

a sip of iced-cold water
from the fragile tumbler

sensitive as an instep
chimes with
the season of change

the season of dandelion clocks
& the back of an envelope

swallows line the wire
ready for home
its June

rape-seed yellow burns retinas
the field next door
at home its coffee & bananas

echo united
you you you & you
I don't do what you do do I

sat hunched & crumpled
knocked for six

the Essex windmill feathered
motionless
down sunbeams

a muse's arm outstretched
disc of sun emerges
a tambourine

like the lore
dead-eyed as a spread sheet
all measure with a tuning fork

One Last Song

you died into memory

the way you open a door
dance down a flight of stairs

when Poetry was the software

the World was a state
entirely joined together
of consequence

like leaves like
like to like

subject to the logic
or web of argument
the stars

I press "like" browse on
I shouldn't say
fallen to the ground

the minute details in the gone

leaning to the end
breathe together

reading clouds after so long
I could remember you

fizzled or zipped away
to darkness under tables
& cracks

a scooted continuous ending
to come home to

so tired I can't read straight
or stand by declarative statements
the cant

out of date so soon
taking notation

the World in "sleep"
in all its matrices revealed

from the Grand World of Expression
did I join the right line
whilst wearing the wrong shoes

nations on stand by
I shouldn't stay

lines drawn a plan b
as much as a practical solution
left by its mark

for all the World imagined you

details there to be taken in
leading to ending

to meet blue in the horizon

www.ingramcontent.com/pod-product-compliance
Lightning Source LLC
Chambersburg PA
CBHW031634160426
43196CB00006B/414